# 50 poems for my 50ᵗʰ

## A BEGINNER'S GUIDE TO OPENING
## THE WORLD WITH WORDS

## Sarah de Nordwall

*Sarah de Nordwall*

*June 2016*

THE BARD'S SCHOOL

The Bard School Press

*an imprint of*

www.thebardschool.blogspot.com
www.fast-print.net/bookshop

# 50 POEMS FOR MY 50th

Copyright © Sarah de Nordwall 2015
www.sarahdenordwall.com

Cover design by Claire Barrie of Here is My Design
www.hereismydesign.com

A catalogue record for this book is available from the British Library

ISBN 978-178456-234-2

First published 2015 by
FASTPRINT PUBLISHING
Peterborough, England.

*Dedicated to the following family and friends*
*who have encouraged and cajoled*

To Tom Kingsley Jones, who said

'I leave for America the day before your birthday. I will not leave
the house without a copy of your poems in my hand.'

To Kevin Turley, who said

'If you do not publish your poems before your birthday, I will not
come to your party'

To my dad, Tony de Nordwall, who left this world on 15th
December 2014 and who, although he will not ever have this book
in his hand, will be enjoying it from a wholly different perspective.
And this was always one of his particular talents.

To the Bards of the Bard School and all other indispensable
encouragers in my life, who love to see others shine,
including particularly

Biddy de Nordwall and Janey de Nordwall
Tamara Gal-On, Neil and Fiona Blackley and the Dallys
Miles Blackley, Judith Howard, Edmund Adamus
Sarah Myers, Sarah Larkin and Shirley Embleton
Hugh and Louisa Preston, Sally Baily, Jenny Lochner
Teresa and Phil Loy and Bernadette Barrett
Tom Bentall, Helen Munt, Danielle Welsh, Claire Barrie
Rosy Hosking, Denise Hosking and Margie Brauer
Jim and Lisa Anderson, David and Elaine Chalmers-Brown
Charlotte Bromley-Davenport and Justin Harmer-Harper
Alice Robertson, Marco Storz, Ruth Davies
Bess Twiston-Davies, Dawn Eden, Kitty Turley
Fr Hugh Mackenzie, Fr Dominic White, Msgr Keith Barltrop
Fr Richard Nesbitt, Fr Dominic Robinson and Fr Tom Smith

# Endorsements

'Sarah has a powerful way of tending to life - to the hearth in my heart. I have become re-inspired to take up the desire to become an advocate of beauty, to become a Bard who, without fear, will speak truth to the world through simple dedication of my dream and an attentive presence. Sarah has reminded me what literature is and what it can look like. Poets, like bees, are the smallest of creatures, but they make the sweetest of things.

The Bard School is much needed in our world today. We need these voices speaking out truth into the storm of confusion – we need to hear once again the voice of the Bards.'

Tyrrell Hiatt, Yellowhead County, Alberta, Canada. Bard of the Bard School in Bruno, Saskatchewan May 2015

'Jam-packed with humour and jam-packed with theology'

Revd Rob Gillion, Diocesan Bishop of Riverina, New South Wales, Australia, in whose Church in Knightsbridge, London, Sarah was Bard in Residence from 2003-2005

'Listening to Sarah's poetry is a privilege, but now being able to read it, the experience is even more exquisite, intimate and enchanting. My favourite of her poems is the first of her collection because it is an exemplar of Sarah's life.'

Thomas Kingsley Jones, BA (Dunelm) Bayswater, London, UK, who was manager of Sarah's Poetry Shows and Creativity to Contemplation workshops 2014-2015

# Contents

# Sarah's Introduction

The most motivating reason to publish poetry, is for a party. I'm sure that Bilbo Baggins would agree.

As would that most celebratory of all philosophers, Joseph Pieper, whose name is pronounced Peeper. And isn't that an excellent name for a philosopher, whose job it is to keep Looking Into Things? He was the one who responded to that most important question of Hölderlin's, "What use are poets in times of distress?" This was one of his answers –

*"Anything that festively raises up human existence, the arts, derive their life from a hidden root, which is contemplation, which is turned towards God and the world in order to affirm them.*

*All that exists carries somehow the imprint of paradise, and all authentic arts, the offspring of the Muses, exist to make this truth transparent."*

So there it is, in black and white; Poetry exists for the purposes of festivity, affirmation and the revelation of paradise – and all of this, springs from contemplation.

1

As a great lover of science fiction, I have always dreamed of books that take one from one end of the universe to, at least, the end of another; universes both inner and outer, being implied. So in this poetry book, I have included enough stepping stones from the Trilogy of my Poetry Shows, to take you from the world of 'Lipstick is a Spiritual Experience', through 'The Universe was Not at Home' to 'The Best things in Life are a Waste of Time'.

I hope that there will be enough of your favourites there to take you into a world in which you find enchantment.

For enchantment is a wonderful and a necessary thing; both peace-filled and perilous, wild and free.

It was Stratford Caldecott, that most gentle and insightful of commentators on Tolkien, who described the word 'enchantment' as meaning, 'To be placed inside a song'. This interpretation he drew from the French words 'en' and 'chant' - 'inside' and 'song'.

For this is what a poet hopes to give you in a poem – a moment of magical transportation. So that you may find yourself not only experiencing the marvellous feeling of being somehow inside a song, but perhaps even encountering the great Singer of all the Songs and becoming yourself inspired to sing an even more beautiful song. For, as Joseph de Maistre the philosopher said,

'Reason speaks in words alone, but love has a song.'

And now we are ready to begin.

**1.**

**I put an orchid in my room**

I put an orchid in my room
When the room was a total mess.
The orchid was so beautiful
She had the power to bless.

And all the things in plastic bags
That were stacked against the wall,
Beneath the grace of her perfect poise
Were needed not at all.

I put an orchid in my room
A single still white flower.
Disorder left and chaos fled.
Her loveliness was power.

1999

**2.**

## Lipstick is a Spiritual Experience

Red makes me look yellow
And pink makes me look green.

My lipstick is important
I need something in between.

It can't be purely vanity
My lipstick aids my sanity.

It has a very spiritual role;
Its colour evokes my eternal soul

Cos only one shade will be just quite right.
The conclusion is an axiom; depth prevents it being trite

That on the Boots cosmetics shelf
I can seek the key to my inner self.

Is it, 'Dew Bright Delight' or 'Extreme Red Sensation'
Perhaps 'Pastel Pretension' or 'Unglossed Revelation'?

Yes, Lipstick is poetry.  Truth, held in plastic,
Enhanced on the base with descriptions fantastic.

I love it, I love I can't do without it
It's just quintessential, there's no doubt about it.

When I camped in Arizona and alas forgot the water,
I brought along my 'Rouge Extreme', Chanel
From Mama to daughter.

No, it's not one of those fetishes or self-created needs
It's an aspect of one's vital flow without which life recedes.
Yes, it's purely existentially I feel the need is there
To be a lip-sticked feature on the front of 'Marie Claire';

A Platonic ideal with a full lipped appeal
A New Age dawn in 'Promiscuous Prawn'-
The contemporary pink that can make a woman think.

'Escape', 'Obsess', 'Conceal' 'Reveal',
No it's not all the same, it's not just in the name
Categorically real, it's a knowledge you feel.
So go out and try - Get up and buy!

Make over your make up and feel your soul fly

Don't stick to old habits

Throw your old tubes away

Get down to the chemist and find the way!


Now, you may choose 'Electrica' or

'Entirely New Hue',

But whatever may reflect your Self

Make sure it's wholly You!


1994

**3.**

**Time will Tell**

I never heard Time speak.
She holds her cloak around her secrets.

Sometimes, perhaps,
She lays her picnic blanket
On the ground,
But I provide the food
As do those who might pass by.

I never heard Time singing
Though the trees she nurtures, who contain her presence
Hold the birds who sing.

They sense that love is in the branches
And that all around
Came once from one whole good,
Which they rejoice in.

I never heard Time sigh
But as events and people peer from billboards
Tabloids, postcards, windows,

Anguished faces, shouts of joy,
I bring a lover's eye
To every sight
And seek the Lover's glance
In all the Guernica and Jubilee.

I never heard Time speak.
Her silence, though, invites response.
The only guarantee
Perhaps, is that Time listens.
That is telling.

What does she hear
In me?


11<sup>th</sup> August 2005

**4.**

For Colin

## Microwave Man

They say little creatures crawled out of the slime
And became human beings in a matter of time,
So that, that which once wallowed in primeval bogs
Now thrives in society's civilised cogs.

Which cog you engage with, you choose, if you can
And one I've encountered is Microwave Man.
Society's lubricant, money, he earns
In generous quantities,
Thus his cog turns.

And he's almost concerned that his own cog has teeth
Which might possibly grind other cogs underneath.
But as he's no mechanic,
In fact he's in banking
He won't ask awkward questions for which
No one would thank him.
So he just relaxes with the things he enjoys
Innovations and wonderful new high-tech toys.

He's got a laser-light pen that shines red on the wall

And a micro-electron storm in a glass ball

And the touch panel sound system's sure to appear

If he gets that nice bonus at the end of the year,

No, he'll get it now, on next year's fee

Cos he can get it on credit

So it feels like it's free..

Soon each switch is remotely controlled at whim

He can turn on the microwave from the home gym.

And all of his friends come round to play

As the gadgets pile up from day to day.

They're so well designed,

Yes his friends think they're great,

They're an absolute joy to contemplate.

But there isn't much time to enjoy them really

Cos he gets home late and he's at work early.

The firm wants more and he's at home less,

So he works a little harder and he starts to feel the stress.

And he's almost tempted to get a bit upset

When there's no one at home to talk to but the wide screen TV set.

And he wonders if a holiday might feel nice on his own

But he can't quite yet afford it, so he thinks about a loan.

He could sell a couple of gadgets..

Aah, they're not yet his to flog,

And he starts to envy creatures that just wallow in a bog.


So he pierces the film of his plastic tray meal

And he microwaves Full Power

But he must have got distracted

Cos he leaves it in an hour


And as he watches his well-nuked food

In electric light revolve,

He wonders,

Cosmologically,

'What does it mean,

Evolve?'

**5.**

## Microwave Man's Woman

He sought for a sense of the sacred,
For a god he could hold aloft,
And he found her,
Gymnastically raiding tombs,
The virtual, Lara Croft.

With a Cyber Babe Body to challenge the mind
And a mission as firm as her pixelled behind,
She's utterly buxom yet totally slim
And you just turn her on and off, at whim.

So Microwave Man runs home to play
With the babe that won't tire at the end of the day.
As she springs divinely from chasm to pool,
Microwave Man can adventure or drool.

And the graphics are stunning and all in 3D
So who needs a social life or Web TV?
Once Microwave man asked if life had a goal
Now he's happy with Lara Croft's dive forward roll:
So perfectly pleasing, so aesthetically whole,

And you just press the arrow key, shift and control.

It's astonishing really, the joy that you feel
In playing with a woman who is not even real!

So Microwave Man plays by day and by night
Entranced by the screen
Encased like Snow White
Who slept in a coffin of glass
Till Love's kiss
Awoke her to life and a foretaste of bliss.

But Microwave Man needs no lover sublime
He's got objects to find, so he hasn't got time.

So Microwave Man is contented to stay
Close behind Lara Croft
And to watch and to pray.

Bless all the devoted in thy virtual care
And fit us for heaven
To live with thee there.

**6.**

## Rimelda Urban-Mystica

Rimelda Urban Mystica
Conceived the essence well,
Life's call rang out within her
Like a clear Tibetan bell.

When floors were swept
And walls were white
When paper shutters filtered light,
When all her mind was one bright sky,
Her thoughts were clouds which floated by.

Rimelda's posture stilled her soul.
A silent heart
Her single goal.
Slow-filled with lightness as she breathed
Her inner tensions were relieved.

But 20 minutes
Come and gone
The daily doing drew her on.
And though for an hour or two she'd feel

Consumer pressures were less real

Yet she'd look up

With swimming soul:

A small fish in life's goldfish bowl

To surface tension's silver sky

And wish that flying fish

Could fly.


She wondered as she held her broom

What lay beyond Life's temporal room.

In a quantum physicist's particle spin

She'd ask 'Which universe am I in?'


Her Tesco card arrived by post.

She spread the Marmite on her toast,

And spent the morning wondering when

She'd find the reason

For purposeless Zen.


But Zenki mind states emphasise 'Now'

So focus on the 'What' and 'How',

So in the paper

Double quick

She circled appeals for helping the sick..

A course in psychotherapy,

A therapeutic community,

A youth worker training for those who intuit,

The Social Work section

She loved to leaf through it.

Her thoughts, though specific, were rarefied

For Rimelda had never been qualified:

But could she be helpful and counter distress

By raising the world's Higher Consciousness?

In the Mystical Body or One World Soul

A purified input

Could be her role!

She suddenly sensed a renewal of energies,

Found a review of the Top Ten Zen Monasteries,

And prayed that though Buddhists say "All is One"

She could still worship God

As second to none,

And sealing the letter in which she'd applied

She tinkled her wind chimes with mystical pride

And beaming within at the urban sprawl
Gave thanks to the spirit and maker of all

And off to the post box she ran with zeal
Intent on her mission
To reach
For the real.


1995

**7.**

## Felicity Fastrack

Felicity Fastrack, neat as Nietzsche
'Overman', had nought to teach her.
A girl on top, with a mind to match her
Fewer U turns than Margaret Thatcher.

She had it all
And delivered it too
She was GQ IQ babe, come true.

Wagner's Valkeries lulled her dreams
And Mighty Mythos fanned her schemes..
Taxless freedom, choice and power,
Chance to thrive
But first, devour,
Jungle-juice-adrenaline-pushy,
Survival of the adamant
Who scorn the soft and cushy.

Greatest is who greatest does
Shift the product
Feel the buzz

Drive the sheep for their own sake
Strive and seek through fire and quake.

Joan of Arc herself would quail
In her armour, look but pale
Next to Felicity
Crème de la Crème
Fast-Tracked into fantasy
With plans no facts could stem.


1998

**8.**

## The Universe was Not at Home

The Universe was not at home,
I was knocking on and on
I said, 'Universe, you've got to be in
Or else where the hell else have you gone?'

But the Universe was not at home,
'Gone out for a jaunt, I suppose,
But what's to become of the rest of us now?
Well, only heaven knows'.

I tried to complain
It was just no good
Cos Space was out of his head
And Time was late
He said, 'Blame it on fate
Or try the World instead'.

I said, 'The World is full of Rock Stars
Who are neither out nor in.
Not only do they not know who they are
You don't know where they've been!

No, I came to find the Universe
But the Universe is out.

I'd like to complain
I'll be back again'
He said, 'Nobody hears when you shout.'

I said 'Time, you're too short to be picking a fight
Can we just simmer down and be friends?
Because what if the Universe never comes back
Slinks off or implodes or just ends?

It's rather alarming, don't you think
With the Universe out, and us on the brink?'

'Look he's not gone away forever, said Time
On a round the space-time curve trip.
There's no such thing as forever in here
I'm Time I should know, take a tip.

It's nice that you missed him
But no need for alarm
He's just out expanding
He'll come to no harm.'

So I stomped off home

And I kicked off my shoes

And I hoped I was too late to catch the news,

But as I was sitting alone in my chair

I suddenly felt the Universe there.

Then I heard him knock

I said,' Where've you been?'

He said, 'Just out visiting

Can I come in?'

I said, 'Who were you visiting

What did you see?'

He said, 'Here are the photos.'

'What?  Here's one of me!

But what an odd angle

You've got a strange eye.'

He said, 'I'll leave it with you then,

Got to fly.'

I said, 'Leave me your number!

What shall I do?'

He said,' Don't ring me love
I'll ring you.'

So the Universe is not at home
But the picture recalls the day
When I was at home with the Universe
And he almost came to stay.

But I wonder about that photo -
And what is that light on my face?

I must have looked straight at the camera
But all I could see was just space.


1997

**9.**

**Wondering what I'm talking about**
Or 'On why your own poems are worth listening to'

The thing about poems is that they go ahead of us.

They've had a look over the horizon, but they aren't telling.
Except in clues and images – the language of dreams.

They always seem to be a little more honest than we are.
A little more knowing.

So when I write, I try not to edit, supress, inhibit.  I just put it
down and type it up, print it off and come back later, to take
a look and wonder; what am I talking about?

And this process uncovers some doors and opens some
locks, that otherwise might never have been found.

Like the secret garden that the child Mary found in the story.
She needed a robin to attract her attention to the ivy, that hid
the rusted lock.  One should always take notice of robins,
because they can fly over the wall.

Robins are soul friends, just like poems. They look quite innocent, but they're hiding something. For fun.
Follow them.

Because they like to play with you.

But what they're hiding, they're also revealing.
Because they know, even if you don't, what you mean to say.


April 2$^{nd}$ 2015

**10.**

Sometimes a poem is a direct result of a prayer to help you speak out against some threat to freedom or to joy. This poem came into my head in just such a way, and began with this wonderful phrase from Paul Hogget's essay on 'The Institutionalisation of Shallowness' from his book 'Partisans in an Uncertain World'. He was describing the type of leaders who disempower others and who, in order to perpetuate their reign, become 'The Container of Abandoned Minds'.

I performed the resulting poem for the UN Rapporteur on Freedom of Conscience and Belief, who was visiting the House of Lords, to listen to a range of submissions from groups in the UK, who had something to say about freedom of speech. My plea was for an end to the shutting down of discourse through the use of politically correct and standardised language, that smuggles in ideology and closes down debate.

It did rather change the atmosphere in the room.

## The Container of Abandoned Minds

There is a place
Where standardised thought
Will lead, if you care to go.
Why so few see, where the path leads on
Is hard to say, or know.

The road takes little effort
As it slopes and twists and winds.
But when you arrive, you'll know the place;
The container of abandoned minds.

Its walls are sheer consensus
Their surface, entirely flat
They almost seem to absorb the light
They're so utterly grey and matt.

And all the sounds are deadened
The many voices, stilled

For the Container of Abandoned Minds
Is crushingly, shockingly filled.

Its inhabitants are all relieved
Of the strain of a complex life,
Where grace and suffering mend the world
And receive the surgeon's knife.

No healing there,
Through pain or joy
They are offered this instead;
That all the world become the same
And the living obey the dead.

There is a place
Where standardised thought
Will lead, if you care to go.

The container of abandoned minds
Don't say you didn't know.

2009

**11.**

Poetry is not just for the opening of the eyes to danger, but the opening of the heart to wonder.

This is a poem I wrote as a thank you card for Kitty's uncle Charlie, who lent us his enchanted house in France for a week one summer. On his desk was a book on astronomy that I loved. And then, there was the garden and the night of the shooting stars.

### The Garden at 'La Villette'
*On the night we sat back in deck chairs, as the night fell and all the shooting stars came out to play*

The garden like a cradle hangs
Suspended in deep space.

The lawn, by day, that sweeps down to a friendly grove
Is now a curving precipice
On which we all tilt forwards and risk
A fall into the great abyss.

But now we all rock back again
And tilt together at the shooting stars.

These sparks from the galloping hooves of Pegasus
Awaken us to the drama of the skies
Imagining the rush of wild Andromeda
A hundred miles a second towards her suffering child.

Our Galaxy approaches hers at this tempestuous pace
Till noble Pegasus, the winged horse, dives in victory
Towards the sea-beast in a tide of stars.

One day our galaxies will wholly merge
And quieten every sword.
The drama of the heavens
Tells the glory of the Lord.

But now the arm of this our Milky Way
Protects us with a quiet, maternal care.

She knows we tend to wander off;
A hundred million years to lose our way.
A hundred million more to make it home.

And all around us, light flies forth,
Three hundred trillion metres every second
To tell us of the stars that sing

Nine million light years hence.

But when these messengers of light arrive,
The stars they left have fled from us
Full eighty five million light years hence
Accelerating from us, ever more,
By which strange force, no human person knows.

They call that energy 'dark', by which this
'All that is' still grows.

Above the quince and the walnut trees
I saw the curve of earth in La Villette.

The gentle lawn pretends its pleasant sweep;
But let the night time fall!
And feel the Earth,
Precipitous,
Up end us
Into
Awe.

Summer 2012

**12.**

First lines, nicked from other people's poems, can be such a juicy starting point for a poem, that I can happily encourage you to borrow the first line of this one, which I've invited many people to write with and they've come up with some marvellous poems. So go on! You really can try this at home and then let me know how you get on. The line is 'The Edge of our Unknowing'.

Here's my poem, which ended up being about friendship. You never can tell where poems are going to take you. Sometimes you just have to trust, and not think too hard. It's also fun to write alongside other people and that's what happened here. So this poem is for Tom Kingsley Jones, because one day he said that it was time to write poems and then said, 'What about?' and I said, 'I always try to write from the edge of my unknowing', so he said, 'Good, let's write about that then. Go!' And so we did.

## The Edge of Our Unknowing

I like it that friendship is like getting into a boat
Pushed out from the shore.

There'll always be more
You want to know
To see, to feel, to sail
But there's only the journey
Never arriving
But the sea is wide and free.

I like it that friendship is like getting into a boat
And you wish it was made of glass

Because then you would see the fish at night
In their own sweet world.
The secret thoughts of that other mind
In a universe oblivious to your own being
And yet so vast and real.

But sometimes the fish look up
And the wood is glass-like.

A sudden seeing from a light beyond
A glimpse in the line of sight
And the sight is a distant shore
But it comes with a promise.

Why such familiarity in the shared vision?
Why such security in a fleeting gaze?
Such delight that the unknown way is prepared around us
And this ever-expanding freedom is uniquely ours.

I like it that friendship is like getting into a boat
In a world of wonder.

2nd February 2015

**13.**

At another time, I was on an island with my jazz pianist
friend Tom Bentall and we were sitting quietly looking at the
sea.

## With Tom on the Island of Bol, in the cove below the Monastery

There are layers of blue in the grey mist
Sea coloured sky coloured
Wave and deep down pebble coloured
All is one before me.

Pine trees, lightening lime and needle green soft
Tender, spiked at tip
Grace wind-bent trunks
Offering bundled foliage with a
Sheltering care
And underneath
Their shade
We watch the Pirate ship with empty masts
Balance slyly
Along the sharp fine line of the horizon.

**14.**

I travelled once more to Croatia, to an island at the westernmost end of the archipelago. I selected it for the simple reason that I had heard there was a church there called 'Our Lady of the Pirates'. And so, one night at midnight, I arrived by boat and met a man who showed me around the island, when all the world was asleep.

**'Our Lady of the Pirates'**

I saw the Oleander and the Tamarisk tree beside the shore.

You took me there at night,
Where the shutters of the old stone houses
Creaked with age beneath the yellowing moon.

Our Lady of the Pirates – what a tale you told
Of the old church
At the far point of the bay
As we came to the stone well.

The pirates, many years ago,
Had stolen a painting of the Mother of God.

Their ship had sunk
And all that was drawn up from the wrecked boat
Was this image.

When the fishermen carried it here
And placed it on the ground
A spring burst forth
And here the well was built and now the church.

The image in the candle-lit interior
Is enhanced by many prayers
In polyphonic voices richly sung
By fishermen and women dressed in black.

I wonder that the pirates had the nerve.
How little must they then have known
Of how the universe was woven

As another fisherman's poet wisely said
'Of a thread too bright for the eye'.

Take now into your hands this simple cloth
Your life, the one you weave
Of hempen homespun or of gold

And as we sit and spin our tale
Feel tenderly the texture of this cloth
Beneath your hand

And seek within its warp and weft
The thread too bright for the eye,
Divinely planned

For as the last door opens and you leave this world of time
This cloth will be the robe you wear
As the last bell chimes.


July 15th 2006


The other fishermen's poet mentioned in this poem is
George Mackay Brown, the Orkney poet and this line
appears in his poem 'Shroud'.

**15.**

When the sacred comes home, the well springs forth.

Writing a poem can be like a sacred moment and a coming home, from which much else can spring;   life, energy and a sense of renewal.

This is why poems can be vital in moments of decision.

Writing them can help you to know what you really feel. You can sometimes sense the image pointing out the path ahead. The next two poems are both about deciding to leave different organisations. Without the poems, I don't think I'd have found the door.

**I will go out now**

My heart is heavy with the weight of complicity
And I will weave no more
Where the weft is warped so darkly

And the straw we would have spun to gold
Is straw still at the last
And breaks in my hand

And cuts my fingers till they bleed

I will go out now
And I will wash my hands in a mountain stream
And I will touch again the face of the sky
And I will touch again the face of the child

And I will leave no stain behind
And I will leave no trace
Behind.


August 1999

**16.**

**I must leave you**

I must leave you
By the fountain
By the garden's inner wall
I shall close the door behind me
So I cannot hear you call.

I look towards the mountain
Though the mountain looks so far
But you are so much further from me
Sitting where you are.

I must leave you
By the fountain
By the garden's inner wall
I shall close the door behind me
So I cannot hear you call.

I'm sorry if the jungle
Is the garden that I seek
I would bring exotic flowers
But I fear they would not keep.

You watch me, unprotected, leave
To walk this vagrant course
And you sit beside the fountain
But I seek the fountain's source.

I must leave you
By the fountain
By the garden's inner wall
I shall close the door behind me
So I cannot hear you call.

I leave, but must I lose you
You could follow
Will you come?
But the door is locked behind me
And is silent
It is done.

I walk towards the mountain
Till I hear another cry
The waterfall calls distantly
And I run beneath the sky.

**17.**

## Falling into Beauty

I often wonder whether I should
Leap into the sea.

I like leaping better than planning.

Maybe it's just fortunate that
I get caught by dolphins
Rather than rocks.

But maybe it's the Way of Things
The Way it's meant to be
In a world of freedom
A world made safe by God.

I'm not saying stupidly
Leap into anything.
You have to wait for the Push
The word of Command
But when it comes
You'll know the sound

Silently

And loud as church bells
Tenderly

And wild as the imperative needs of war

The call will come
And you

Will leap.

**Part Two**

From where I am
I can see the future like a fire work display.
It's bright and dazzling
And it's springing out of the dark,
But how to get there?

I always knew I ought to plan things better
But when I do, my knowing shrinks
Till I can't quite see the forest

Or the floor.

There's always more I can't discover
And I start to hedge and run for cover

No

I'm listening

That's the way

You'll send an elf friend
Down the elven way
And there we'll meet
When I've begun the journey

And I am sure
I know the way

From here.

21st March 2015

**18.**

I'm not sure that I was always so positive about what lay beyond precipices, but I do remember the moment when it all turned around. And this is a story with a poem at the end of it. Although it appears in my CD 'Lipstick is a Spiritual Experience' I think I'd like to tell it here, because in everyone's life, (especially if you've reached a Halfway to Heaven Birthday as I have), it's good to look back and remember the fulcrum moment; the point about which everything turned, when you reached out on an inspiration and were extraordinarily affirmed in a way you could never have imagined possible. For the 'Yes' came from a realm that you had imagined was merely somewhere over the rainbow and yet was in fact more real by far, than anything you had yet encountered. So here, for your contemplation, is the entirely true story of the Hermits. May their blessing be with you in all the regions of the earth in which you dwell.

One day, someone left a book outside my door. On the cover it said 'Holy Daring, an outrageous gift to modern spirituality by the grand wild woman of Avila' – and inside the cover someone had written 'Saw this and thought of you' – but the first chapter looked promising – it was about '*Duende*' – the deep dark passion of the soul – the essence of Flamenco.

And I thought 'oh yes'! The second chapter, as far as I can remember was about Hermits, but the third chapter appeared to be about Flamenco dancing hermits who live in a wood in Nova Scotia and who take a vow of leisure – and I thought 'Oh Yes!!

I **have** to go there'.

I wasn't put off by the fact that they lived in silence and in solitude. I simply knew I had to go. But I didn't have any money and was in a job in Fetter Lane which tells you all you need to know about the job. And the salary was about as liberating, but I thought 'Never mind!' – and just by chance I got a phone call from a cousin who said – 'You know, Sarah, I just got a feeling that you're meant to go and spend some time in Solitude and I said 'Well it's funny you should mention that because I've just been reading about some Flamenco dancing hermits who live in a wood in Nova Scotia and who take a vow of leisure and I was thinking of going there' and she said 'Oh YES!!!'

So I rang international directory of enquiries and I asked them if they knew anything about the flamenco dancing hermits who live in a wood in nova scotia and take a vow of leisure and they said 'Well, there's a post office about 40 miles away from there, so why don't you fax them there and see if they reply?' So I did.

I faxed the hermits.

And they faxed me back.

My boss at the time received the fax.

He said 'There's a fax here from a post office in Nova Scotia, that says the bears are definitely asleep in the winter and the hermits are willing to receive visitors.. Sarah, I'm assuming it's for you and I said 'Oh YES!!!!'

Well that was it, I had to go! So, all that remained was the question of the money. But, as life would have it, I got a phone call from a lovely friend from Kansas and I told her about my plan and she said 'Look, I'm an air hostess and I get 6 free buddy passes a year and you can have one!'

So then I was terrified because I really **had** to go.

Now, I'd never spent any time, as far as I could remember, either in solitude or in silence and so three weeks in a log cabin alone in a wood suddenly seemed an alarming prospect, so I went to consult with my friend John, who is a forensic mental health social worker, who is just the kind of friend every girl should have and I told him about my now imminent plan of going to live in silence and solitude with the flamenco dancing hermits who live in the wood in nova scotia and who take a vow of leisure and I asked what I should take with me. How should I prepare? And he said 'Sarah, if you're going to encounter the void, encounter the void'.

And I thought 'He gets paid to give advice like that. I'm in the wrong job.' So, with no books, cassettes (this was 1996) or home luxuries of any kind except some new thermal underwear, I boarded the plane to Eastern Canada. Well, I have to say that I was so nervous about the whole idea, that as the plane was descending, I started to hyper ventilate and had to be taken off the plane in a wheelchair (after it had landed) but I thought 'Never mind…heroism has to begin somewhere'. But then a new obstacle arose in my mind.
I thought, 'How am I going to know who has come to pick me up at the airport?'

But then, as if by a miracle, I just *knew* that it was the person with the long beard, the brown tunic and the sandals. And he took me off in his pick-up truck and drove me into the woods.

Night had fallen. But as soon as I arrived, I knew it was a Good Wood. And he handed me a little hurricane lamp, and led me down to my little hermitage, which was by the side of a frozen lake.

The hermitage was perfect – it was made entirely of wood and on the veranda were stacked piles of logs – all frozen.  It was at this point that he mentioned that there was no actual heating in the hermitage, other than the wood stove, which I would have to keep alight day and night, otherwise I might die, so there was my motivation for learning how to light a fire.  And there was no running water, but there was a well a little further on into the wood and I could go to the well and break the ice with a stick and draw up my water.

Well I was delighted. The next morning I got up at 4.30am because that's the time you get up when you're a hermit. And kneeling on the patchwork quilt on my bed I looked out through the little window at the stars above the frosty pine trees and I could see that snow had fallen.

At this I leapt from my bed and rushed out through the door and headed down to the frozen lake – I rushed back, put on my thermal underwear and five other layers of clothing and rushed back out and found a little boulder down by the side of the lake.

Well, just a little tip, if you do ever decide to settle down on a boulder at the side of a frozen lake in the winter in Nova Scotia; expect to be there for quite a while because you can get stuck. However it was worth the inconvenience because as I sat there in the stillness, I suddenly heard an extraordinary sound – a deep, dark kind of groaning and creaking, as though a monster were trapped under the ice, but then I realised it was the ice cracking and moaning like the primeval beasts of legend.

As I sat there transfixed, I noticed something else. The lake was gradually turning lilac, until a thin shaft of gold shot across the surface, as though a door had opened in heaven.

It was the dawn and gradually, as the sun rose, the door from heaven opened and the gold spread out across the lake.
And then – I could hardly believe what I was seeing – the air itself started to sparkle in a myriad of colours and I realised that the air itself must be frozen and reflecting the coming of the light prismatically....

Well, as I say, I sat there doing nothing but be amazed for some hours and I reflected that in London, when I am mainly running around in a day rammed with activities, I spent a lot of the day feeling rather empty, but there, in Nova Scotia, with absolutely nothing to do, I felt absolutely full.

And that is how it went on.

The woods were my own and I explored them as though I had arrived on a pristine planet and my freedom was as unbounded as my joy.

One night however, at about midnight, there was a knock on my door, which is odd when you're a hermit. And there, outside, was a woman with two pairs of ice-skates on her shoulders and she said, 'The moon is up'.

And I thought, 'Maybe that's how you talk, when you're a hermit', and I was unsure how to reply, but she added, 'Come with me to the lake!' So I followed after her until we reached the edge and she began to explain – 'At the edge of the lake the ice is thin. In the centre of the lake the ice is thick. So we are going to walk along this log in these ice skates and when we get to the end, we will jump and zoom.'

I paused slightly. It would have seemed churlish to mention that it had been many years since I had put on ice skates and that, at that time, there had been no mention of icy logs, cracking ice or jumping and zooming, but I reflected that I hadn't come all that way to make excuses and so I obeyed, laced up the skates, wobbled along the log and before I knew it, had jumped and zoomed..

And there we suddenly were, skating under the bright moon through the thin layer of snow on the wide, white moonlit lake and on and on we skated till the moon began to set.

Well, after this experience and many unforgettable times spent sitting round the great oval table on the Sabbath day, when the hermits would meet together and we would drink from the goblets they had fashioned themselves and talk and talk of wonderful things and they would sing their songs beside the great fire - after all this, I truly thought that not only was I utterly transformed, but that life could never ever be the same again..

But when I got back to London, I remembered that I now had no job and no money and it was time to find something to do. So feeling that at least I might go and embark on something worthy, I made my way down to Knightsbridge to the Charity Recruitment Agency that just happened to be beside Harrods and very soon I was getting quite excited, telling them how fast I could type and how well I could file and organise and before I knew it, the interview was over and I had found myself wandering into Harrods and spending a large amount of the money I hadn't actually earned yet and suddenly I remembered – 'Oh no! I'm meant to be in the Cathedral for a talk on Silence and Darkness'. And then I realised. The great process of my spiritual and material integration as a balanced human being had evidently not been completed. And I was distressed, but not for long, because I thought, 'I know! In order to find out what I really think and to work out what to do, I shall write a poem'. And this is what I wrote..

## I have Opened my Mind to the Drawing of Water

I have opened my mind to the drawing of water.
I have opened my heart to the burning of wood.
In the cold I have felt all the warmth of necessity
Healing a history of ought, must and should.

In the darkness of morning I opened my soul
To the happiest feeling of grasping no goal
And warmed by the fire and chilled by the well
In a passive love action fell under God's spell.

But now in the city the neon is bright,
Though much I encounter is spiritual night.
When safe in a desert of wilderness peace
I watched while the pressured worked hard for release.

Though debts and impatience may urge me to act
I'll not risk my heart in a compromise pact.
Not until inner silence is stronger than din
When prestige appals me and status wears thin

Only then I'll be safely released to the world
Not brandishing ego with CV unfurled.

There's joy in the knowing I learnt to adore
And wait for the summons.
This less is much more.


1995

**19.**

Even when I had decided that the 'less was much more', it was still difficult to stay with that decision over the years.

Occasionally a poem appears to keep me on the path. This was one that seemed to come out of nowhere, when I woke up one morning and simply wrote it out. It still makes me smile.

**I, Caterpillar**
**or Refusing the Cocoon**

The cocoon is a small restricted place
That hangs from a perilous thread.
It looks like a white sarcophagus
And appears to contain the dead.

I, caterpillar, I refuse the cocoon.
Why should I submit?
To trust to a thin and silken yarn,
And reduce my Self to an It?

I've heard the tales of fantasists
Who dream by the light of the moon
Of bright-winged transformations;
'Gifts and Abilities, Coming Soon!'

I laugh, I caterpillar, clearly see
Right through the credulous mind.
I have a grasp of the central theme;
I refuse the ties that bind.

I choose my freedom in my way
No darkling chamber mine.
I see the light on my spots and spikes
And I think they're rather fine.

I glance with pity
Now and then
At those who close themselves in
And make their lives so limited.
What is it they seek as they spin?

I won't hang around to watch them die
And see their forms decay.
I've leaves to eat on other trees.
No death for me today!

He fled from the sound of the krackening,
From the opening of the tomb.
He had turned away
When miraculous wings
Emerged from the dark cocoon.

But as he sat on his laden branch
Where he had grown quite fat,
A shimmering creature dazzled in flight.
"My word, he gasped,
Who's that?"

April 2009

**20.**

And so, that morning when I set off for my first business enterprise class, with the encouragement of the hermits from Canada in my memory, I was planning to learn how to earn a living with no more than a handful of poems. But I felt a little daunted by my reluctance to become either Felicity Fastrack or Rimelda Urban Mystica and I knew as yet of no successful middle way. Fortunately, I decided to ask for a sign. And a sign was given to me, about which I wrote the following poem. And when the going gets tough I read it to myself, to remember when a black sheep ate my business notes.

## A Black Sheep Ate My Business Notes

A black sheep ate my business notes.
I tell you cos it's true.
I went to a business enterprise class
But I ended up in a zoo.

Because just beside Wandsworth Business Village
Lies 'King George's Park"
And with rabbits, canaries and budgies and goats
It's a regular Urban Ark.

And so I dawdled down Cherry Tree Walk
There were no business women or men
So I greeted the goats
But I dropped all my notes
Waving 'Hi!' to the sheep in the pen.

Now the little white sheep just wandered away
But the little black sheep came up to play
And that black sheep ate my business notes
And all my projections and graphs.
But what do you do
With a little black ewe
Who when you mention
Bank accounts, laughs?

I said
"Hey, this is enterprise culture
Not food for the woolly and weak!
I've a living to make
And a profit to take
And a future in credit to seek.

You should be aware of the market place;
It's the world of beef, mutton and ham!
I'd not graze through

As complacent as you

If I were a little black lamb.

But she just nibbled on,

Till my plan was all gone;

Unperturbed, I'd appointments to keep.

I said, 'I'd not expected my first business meeting

To be so delayed by a sheep.'

But Time, it will pass

And I left for my class:

'Next time you want breakfast,

Then just stick to grass.'

But I couldn't forget

That little black nose

As I watched the black hands on the clock.

What *will* become of my business

If it feeds

The black sheep of the flock?

July 1996

**21.**

And so the journey began. At that Business Enterprise Class I met Sarah Myers, who was hoping to become a Tourism Officer. She then got de-railed into becoming a travelling bard with me. And what a joyful time it was. For six years we ate pasta, listened to Dolly Parton and put on poetry shows in art galleries, business conferences, big tops and bars; about the dilemmas we had and the traces of complicated people we encountered, some of whom were lurking inside ourselves. Here are a few of them, who thanks to their poetic emergence, have since been in a much more interesting conversation with each other.

**Natalie Nice**

Natalie Nice did not like vice
She ironed all her creases twice.

Her smile was wide
Her eyes were bright
She knew that she was wholly right.
Her voice was sweet
Her knife was sharp
She thought she'd like

To play the harp.

She always had a lot to say

And taught the world to work and pray

And when she knew you fairly well

She'd warn you off from going to hell

And teach you all the things she knew,

That fear was bad

And so were you.


And thus she did the things she could

And all the things that good girls should.

But Love itself she never found;

The well of love

Dark and profound

From which the living waters flow

Was somewhere that she would not go.


With all her inclinations tamed

Her passions were as yet un-named


And though she giggled,

Seldom laughed

She thought that comedy was daft.


So seriously she smiled

And sighed
And in her secret room
She cried.

1995

**22.**

## The Tale of Libertina and Tidy Trudy

*Chapter One*
*Libertina*

Elizabeth Tina Angelica Jane
Left her school convent and changed her name.
At the age of 16 she had never felt keener,
To take hold of life as the new Libertina.

Determined to live by her own inner light,
She was not up for hearing what others thought right,
'My freedom's my own', Libertina declared
'I'll not cower in a corner as though I feel scared
Cos I feel like a woman who's ready for action.
If you think Michelle Pfieffer's a female attraction,
Then just watch me go,
There's no bar on my door.
I'll try all of those things I was told to ignore,
Yes, I'll sample each one,
Come on mum,
You keep score!

Dear Mother, it's you who has got the psychosis,

You're far too uptight, that's my expert prognosis.

It's simply not healthy, she said with a grin,

To be over obsessed about personal sin.

No, no cautionary tale can now make me relent

Cos I'm ideologically in-de-pen-DENT!

Now Mother, don't tell me that rhymes with 'hell-bent'

Cos your cute little word-games can never prevent

Such a soul as myself from exploring at leisure

The Ways of the World

And the World's Way of Pleasure.

And now that I'm free to test out this approach,

As I'm new to the game, I'll be needing a coach;


But where to begin?

Every choice looks enticing:

Hurrah for the world! Come on, let's do that vice thing'!


So in this frame of mind, Libertina left home

And strode down the road

Very much on her own.

*Chapter Two*
*Tidy Trudy*

Tidy Trudy,

Never moody,

Always nice and nick-named 'Prudy',

Sought with zeal for Love Eternal,

Never read The Woman's Journal.

'Cosmopolitan', did she spurn it?

Ceremoniously burnt it!

Tidy Trudy,

Hot on duty,

Most determined

Fired by beauty.

Loved the smell of Eglantine,

But didn't like to waste her time

And if she wandered in the park,

Would hurry home if it grew dark,

For a walk at night might seem quite casual,

But Trudy feared it might be sensual.


Though the wind through the trees

Stirs like angels' wings,

Elite contemplation is not all it brings

And stirring the heart with creation's effulgence
Was possibly starting to be self-indulgence.

Past the newspaper stand that sold Time Out,
She wondered what Londoners thought about.
Not stopping to buy
She glanced at the sky
And breathed with freedom
As she briskly walked by.

How great to be good
And do just as one should,
What a glorious fate!
Oh no, I'm late!!


1994

**23.**

## Derrick Doldrum

Derrick Doldrum felt he had no role.
He'd been four years on the dole.
With no sense of personal pride,
Contemplated suicide,
But scraping razors down his arm
Had found a purpose in self harm:
It had the power to make him feel
That at least his pain
Was real.

His existence felt absurd
So this action
Was his word.

But the cry of bloody scar
Doesn't get you very far,
If there is no other heart
To interpret this raw art,
So the razors cut more deep
Edging towards
Eternal sleep.

Till perhaps a fate benign
Cut across the final line.
Swift down Little Newport Street
The sound of Tidy Trudy's feet.

Trudy, rushing to Taizé prayer
Trips behind him
Caught her hair
In the toggle of his duffle
Tangles in embarassed scuffle
Soon extracts her hair and band
Hopes he'll kindly understand
'Oh so sorry, terribly rude'
Loses her glasses.
Hyper mood.

Takes his hand
The blood is wet
Latest razor session
Not yet set.

He sees the shudder in her eyes
But can't speak to apologise
Tidy Trudy starts to shake
But Derrick Doldrum

Stares

Awake

Astonished that he's actually done

Something at last to affect someone.


And all is silence

Till almost calm

Tidy Trudy

Takes his arm.


She'll try to be kind

It's the work of the saints

But the smell and the blood are too much

And she faints.


Derrick is dazed

Who's this girl on the ground?

He hears footsteps near by

And he quickly looks round.


And there striding breezily

Devil-may-care

Is a girl who is heading for Leicester Square Fair.


'Oi, Hey!' calls out Derrick

Relieved that he's seen her,

She turns and approaches

'Hi!

I'm Libertina'.


1996

**24.**

Sometimes our salvific moments are wordless. They can spring from the experience of the sacramental world, from nature revealing what lies behind the beauty. It was again in the Croatian archipelago off the coast of the island of Vis that I found a cave that gave me a wondrous glimpse of glory.

**Swimming in the falling star cave**

You can only reach the cave by boat.
I was excited by that.

And once you enter in
You leave the brilliant sun outside

And so, the water, although crystal pure
Is dark,

But all the same, I longed to dive right in.

Just then, I looked up
To a tiny opening in the roof of the cave
Where a ray of light pierced through

And shot like a heavenly visitor
Into the water, with miraculous effect.

The light fell like a falling star
And for some reason no one could explain
Deep in the water, formed a bright green star
That sparkled 15 feet beneath the waves.

I dived into the sea
And swam through cool dark water till I saw the green star
With her luminous blue tail.

And suddenly brilliant light was on my hands.

I, moving through my darkened underwater cosmos
Struck upon this vein of brilliance

Utterly transfigured, all my being flowed with light.
I, joyous, rose up through the water in the star's bright tail
Till bursting through the surface into air
I felt the light fall radiant on my laughing face.

And treading water in this unexpected glory
Laughed again and reached up into light transfiguring
And cried out to the captain of the boat

'Is this how we arrive in heaven,

Emerging from the watery dark whilst following the star

Unique to us?'


The surface of the water, crossed by light,

Refracted on the cave's roof,

Danced with accompanying delight


And I, returning to my boat once more

Moved off into the dark baptismal water of the cave


And from the benediction of the falling star

Found all the sparkling sea, cold on my flesh,

Preparing me for resurrected life

And tingling with the brightening salt of grace.


July 15th 2006

**25.**

I have wondered often, as we all do, why and how such a complex creature as mankind ever came to be. So I asked myself this question as I went to bed one night, and in the morning, as soon as I woke up, this dialogue was running in my head. I had to jump out of bed to write it down before it disappeared.

**The Making of Mankind    or    God and Luci**

**God**        Yes, it'll just be gorgeous!
            Said God, with a gleeful grin.

            All the fun of the flesh, you know,
            With a spiritual life thrown in.

**Lucifer**    Well I think it sounds excessive
            Said Lucifer, what about me?
            Why should THEY have all the best of both
            worlds
            Absolutely free?

| God | Cos Lucifer, they'll love it! |
|-----|-------------------------------|
|     | Just imagine the scene! |
|     | (and God went on for ages, |
|     | He was obviously terribly keen). |

| Lucifer | Well, I think it sounds confusing, (said Lucifer) |
|---------|---------------------------------------------------|
|         | And in bad taste. |
|         | A spiritual animal! |
|         | What's it for? |
|         | I think it's a bit of a waste. |

| God | Oh Lucifer, sometimes you are a bore. |
|-----|---------------------------------------|

| Lucifer | But God, you've made loads of things; |
|---------|---------------------------------------|
|         | Must we have more? |

| God | Oh, *live* a bit, Lucifer, have some fun! |
|-----|-------------------------------------------|

| Lucifer | I've had nothing but stress, since time begun. |
|---------|------------------------------------------------|
|         | What was wrong with eternity? |
|         | Peace and quiet |
|         | Now the whole of creation is an absolute riot |
|         | And what worries me more |
|         | Is it's not over yet. |

I finished those dinosaurs off don't forget.

235 million years!  Honestly God,

I was bored to tears.

They were going nowhere,

Couldn't you see?

**God**      Well they always seemed rather exciting to me.

**Lucifer**    Well now they're extinct and you should be glad.

Admit that some of your plans go bad.

And this latest creation! I have to protest -

I'm concerned.

How could anyone give of their best

Suffused with base matter?

How sluggish!  How twee!

**God**      You've missed the point, Lucifer

Matter is free,

To be wild and transfigured

It's Love's work of art

And now we'll have Man

Who can wholly take part.

*Transumed* in the vibrancy,

Forming anew,

A marvel of marvels!

See, I have thought it through.


Don't think dualistic,

Man will be one.

There'll be no division

Just Love, Life and Fun!

Think of life, lived *through* matter

Where a spiritual act is both love and creation

And matter of fact

And a fact of Matter!

Tremendous!  You'll see!

You'll want to be *in there*!

Are you following me?


**Lucifer**    Well it does *sound* convincing.

But there's more, is that true?

There's always another surprise with you.

**God**     Well Lucifer dearest I do confess

You sometimes amaze me

How did you guess?


Because, Unified Creature

The new earthling life,

I'm going to divide between

Man and wife!

I can't wait to see what they make of that plan.


**Lucifer**     Believe me, said Lucifer darkly, I can.

And there, as you see, is where trouble will start.

I've less faith than you in this hybrid heart.


You're giving too much.

It hasn't a hope.

It'll just overload and then it won't cope.


The theory is great,

But I don't think they'll get it.

And I would suggest that you simply forget it.


**God**     Well, you do have a point, Luce.

But I have a plan!

An angel companion for every man.
Yes Luce, I want you in on this too.
Your angle has helped me to work this through.

In Mankind's psyche you can shed a little light,
Help him see things newly if his worldview gets
too tight
And, sharing their dimensions, you could get a
little taste
Of the matter-spirit unity, and it wouldn't go to
waste!

In fact I like this more and more.
Maybe I could join the team,
In perhaps a wholly physical sense?

| Lucifer | Now hold it, what do you mean? |

I don't even want to imagine
What I think you just implied.
Believe me God, you can count me out.
An angel has his pride.

If you think I'm going to expend my spirit
On some hairy little tyke
You're quite mistaken and out of order.

| God | Well, Lucifer, do what you like. |

But I think Mankind is going to succeed.
Oh come on Luci, do I have to plead?

A toast for Adam and Eve's success..
Oh come on Lucifer, smile and say yes!

| Part II | **Lucifer's proposal** |

I'm sorry, but God is out of control.

It's alarming, but clear to see.

He's embarking on more and more projects
each day
Without consulting me.

What I think it would be wise to do
Is to section him off, on his own
In a place where His schemes can play out to
the full
But He'll chiefly be 'Home Alone'.

He's forever creating scenarios
Where the characters live as they will
And do what they like from morning till night
But, I ask you, who's paying the bill?

Well, it's all of us, angels, who'll have to serve
So Man can live his life of *lurve*

Well I'm sorry.  I think it's a bit of a cheek
You don't see us offered a day off a week.
Yes, I know we've eternity too, to be fair
But just think for a minute, where will it stop?

All God's constructs are complex, ingenious
too

And I think there's some purpose behind it,
don't you?

And I'm more than convinced that He has in
mind
A plan that would leave us way behind.
A project that's simply so absurd
I can't even describe it
I've not got the word.

So what I would suggest
That we do for the best
Is that each of you angels reports
On the things that you see
And relays them to me
And we'll see what old Luci can sort.

Yes I know He's content, but that worries me
too.
It just shows that He can't be thinking things
through.
It proves there must be something amiss.

For instance, what do you make of this?
I clearly confronted Him over His plan

For this matter based spirit that he likes to
call Man
And I asked about purpose?

He said it was 'Love'
And referred to some fantasy friend he called
'Dove'!

It's embarrassing, really.
How much more should we take?
I refer to my first point,
It's for His own sake.

We'll just have him sectioned
In a heavenly home
And hope that He'll learn to see sense
On His own.

Then we can relieve Him of all of the stress;
Take over the Kingdom in a way He would
bless
If He still had the vision
And the structures we need
With responsible roles and a way to proceed.

We need to be sure
what to do and to think
Without all this teetering over a brink
Of explosive potential and passion and risk
It's unbearable!

So, to conclude, let's be brisk.

With the Kingdom our own
And God safe and disarmed,
Our objectives in place,
We can all go unharmed.

Renamed and restructured,
The Kingdom will be such an absolute Haven
You won't need to be free!

Even God will be jealous
Of Our perfect control.
He'll want to be in here, and apply for a role!

But no, seriously,
We'll keep him safely out there,
Cos he'd only upset things,
And it wouldn't be fair.

So, how about a new name

For the Kingdom as well?

It should sound quite like Heaven, but more

punchy,

Yes,


Hell.

**26.**

As my dad used to say when he heard that poem 'We've all worked for people like that.' But in order to escape the mindset that came with working and living in the box, a whole inner journey needed to be undertaken. Because to continue living in such a regimented space, I had absorbed the ideology in the very depths of my psyche, until much that was un-natural felt normal, whilst much that was natural - wild and free, creative and personal – felt almost alien. Learning to live newly can feel very strange indeed, a bit like losing a limb or realising you lost one long ago.

**Ideology**

Dropping an illusion
Is like losing an impossibility -
There's so much potential in it
But at first, there's nothing.

Previously, you realise, you've been using a robotic arm
instead of your own,

Powerful but clumsy,
Un-nuanced in almost every way that mattered.

But now you've let it drop,

You panic -

'That other arm, the one I must have had before

Didn't' I chop it off?'

The metal looked so promising and so worth the sacrifice of flesh and blood.


But you forget.


You reach back in your memory

For a time of natural movement,

A spontaneous touch,

But you can't recall.


Perhaps the arm is somewhere else

Perhaps still with you

Under a coat, unused.


Perhaps it will regrow.

You just don't know

And so

You stop

Unarmed

And wait for freedom.

**27.**

It's a temptation to think that everything, including human behaviour, can be measured and accounted for. Fortunately, the unseen things are often the elements that provide the background to the beauty; the source of their being.

## The Savour

Are we to be condemned for disappointment
As though causality were clear to see
And certainty the goal of intellect -
A spec to put each axis in its place
To measure the coordinates of blame?

Open the imagination
Quest for the question
What is the experience
The savour of compassion?

Is it like basil leaves gladdening the heart
Or the tenderest epiphany of wayside primroses
Or maybe, more the overpowering joy
Of jasmine flowers,
Stopping you mid-stride,

More suddenly than a swerving car?

The door to heaven has been thrust ajar
And all its wildest scents come crashing in.
The death of darkness violently won
And unimagined gifts
So gently given.

May 2004

**28.**

So what went wrong with our eyes upon the world, that we should prefer so often the ugly to the beautiful and the unreal to the real? One day I met a hermit in the woods in Nova Scotia and he said that, maybe, the original sin was not being able to leave anything alone.


**The Wasted Tree**

God said, Enjoy the Sacred Tree
Don't consume it
Let it be

Contemplate the fruit-filled bough
Wonder at beauty, bless and bow
Reverence its inviolate charms
And leave in peace from the grasping arms
The Tree that exists for its sake alone
Not to be a victim of the 'take and own'.

But Eve attended to the Serpent's lie
'It costs you nothing,
Come and buy, for free, what God withholds from you,

He said you'd die. It isn't true.

This tree is wasted. Use it up!

Fill your empty knowledge cup.

Good and Evil you don't know,

But eat the fruit and how you'll grow,

Into Gods

Come on

You'll see.

Only Gods eat from the Wasted Tree.'


'Ooh says Eve, d'you think I should?

Still you're right

It does look good.'


Now kept out of Eden by a flaming sword,

The Serpent is as true

As his slippery word.

For now, consuming night and day

Good and evil come our way

And Eden, where Mankind could play

Becomes the sweat-toil of today.


The Sacred Tree was raped of fruit

We rape the world in a pure wool suit.

And violate the Sacred Day

The Sabbath that was made for prayer and play.

Sacred, useless, life-filled Tree
Save us from Efficiency!

But lo! I hear the sound of feet
Hurrying, scurrying to compete.
The Wasted Tree of Life they seek
To make a good story for 'Start the Week'.

The intellectual appetite needs
New thrills that old religion feeds.

Designer ideas to fill the mind
Out on the airwaves, tuned, refined
No thought unturned, left undefined
Packaged and marketed, PR entwined.

Sacred, useless, Life-filled Tree
Pulped to fiction for the BBC.

What leaf of life can I find of you
That might instruct us what to do?
What leaf-fringed legend might I find
Entreasured in the poet's mind?

Sap of spirit, silent voice
We cannot undo the choice.

Good and evil we received when the Serpent we believed.

Adam lost the Tree of Life
Though complicit, blamed his wife.

Exile we cannot undo,
But the Sacred filters through
Evil we cannot unknow
But can we let the wasted, grow?

Can we listen for the silent sound
Root inviolate
Underground
Simply living,
Growing yet
He who heard
Could not forget

Sacred, Life-filled, Sabbath Free
Shelter us, Oh Sacred Tree!

**29.**

Without the shelter of the Sacred Tree, there are many things
we set out to create which are very far from leading to our
own delight and deepening. I remember reading in 'Wired'
magazine that there was a kind of electronics that was being
developed called moletronics (pronounced mol-e-tronics)
that might allow circuits to be liquid. I didn't really
understand how it could work, but an idea came into my
mind.

**Robotica**

Robotica was dynamite
With moletronic grace
She far exceeded anything
Conceived by the human race.

She shimmered free in 40D
In the planes between dimensions
She fed and fused
Teased and amused
Your higher apprehensions.

Designed by generations of her cyber-kindred kind

She was a neural interface
Within your higher mind.

A digi-spiritual upload
She had the power to cruise
Beyond the mirage of your soul
And there she'd interfuse.
There was no image you'd aspire to
She could not foreknow
No place where you might find yourself
She'd not be first to go.

This ultimate envelopment
It was your prize to keep
And you were her reward as well
In her
Eternal sleep.


2000

**30.**

And yet, far from diminishing in pace, the creation of immersive technologies continues, as though reality is to be found more satisfying as we distance ourselves from the natural world. And so, even in the realm of man and woman, we seek to solve the problems that arise, not by human methods but by tampering with matter and attempting to remove the distinctions between us. Projecting this idea far into the future, I wrote a reflection by an imagined historian, who is looking back from a very different society, in which women do not exist at all, and even men are far from recognisable.

**The Historian's Tale, 5041 AD**

They say there was a type of human

Aeons of the ancient world ago

Whom they called 'Woman'.

Who remembers why,

But it is rumoured,

It was something like a goddess

And connected, if it can be properly believed

With the bringing forth of life itself.


You ask me who believes such folly

Or how could such a strange thing be?

But there are stranger things

Than we can see

Through science or philosophy.


There was a word used to describe this human;

'She'

And in her body,

Do not be alarmed,

There was a living place

Where human life could form.


No, no, 'She' wasn't a machine.

The strange thing was,

This life was personal.

'She' was not a vessel,

But most intimately made,

To be so sensitive,

That something called relationship

Was possible for her.


Yes, even with the tiniest things.

They say, in legend, even with

The Unseen things.


I speak a heresy, I know

*'All things detectable by our machines*

*Are all there is*

*And these we take*

*And forge them to our purposes'*

I know our creed.


And yet

I cannot help but wonder at the fact

'She' was not forged by us.

No, no, I can assure you

'She' was not conceived by man.


You are astounded

Yet, if tales be true

The strangeness pushes further on.


Beyond the coming of the perfect androgyne

And the Many Gendered, now Ungendered race,

There was a time when humans had

A chance

To look at Otherness in a human face


And all was not constructed in an image

We'd defined.


There was a moment when our thoughts went upwards

Outwards, inwards,

Who can say to where

But how I long to find..


I am a shape that's built for no one.

I can only dream

That somewhere in the ancient past

There was a place where we, as humans

Knew there was a

Mystery

In between.


What's that,

my children?

Ah indeed, those old, forbidden words.


Do not erase the words I speak

For when they take me, old historian

No one will know the secret

That was left behind

But you.

22nd March 2014

**31.**

**Reductionists and Sadists**

Reductionists and sadists
Get the same thrills
They're only really happy
When the spirit blood spills.

1997

**32.**

So what is the antidote, if we are to resist a diminishment in our being and a disappearance of our humanity? The answer lies I believe in something I was made to think about by a man on a goat farm some years ago; a certain ancient curiosity about how far this 'being' thing really goes.. both down and up..

## On Trying to get the 12 Levels of Being Through Security

A man on a goat farm in Israel had told me
About a rabbi
Who knew everything
about the 12 levels of being.
I sensed they were badly needed here in London.

So when he went to the Holy land again I asked him to bring them back for me.
He was worried about getting them through security.

And indeed they spotted him with repentance in his rucksack.
She was sewn deep into the lining – the tenth level of being.

But repentance had burst through, revealing

The capacity to create –

The eleventh level.

There for all to see.

 But would they?

It was a tense moment by the conveyor belt.


And still they searched for the twelfth.


When you tried to pass through customs

They sensed you had something to declare.

Did you really think that no one would notice your lack of

the customary reticence?

Did you not think that your unbounded spontaneity would

act as a kind of a giveaway?

'If he is carrying the 12th level of being, we will have to be

very careful.'

They were told on their security warning system


'He is not like one of us

He is utterly incomparable.

He is beyond the furthest horizon of our imagining.

He is off the scale of our comprehension.

 We have merely known the shallows of the mighty deep.'

And so they searched the soles of your shoes to avert an
explosion of joy
They shook out your gloves for something to grasp onto
But your intellectual depths were incapable of detection
By the penetrating scanning of their implacable machines.

Resolved into simplicity and sheer invisibility
You revealed only tenderness in the sublimity of your smile

They mistook your comprehension for stupidity
And foolishly
They let you through.


November 2010

**33.**

## Push aside the Terror of Things to be Done *

Push aside the terror of things to be done;

They were deceivers, ever.

They catch at you without context

Claiming territory

Without treaty

On Sacred ground.


Push aside the terror of things calling

Clamouring from the four corners

Claiming the floor

Where He had brought you to dance

To laugh, to sing, with Him

Alone.


But the things

Trip you

They know that appeasement

Knocks you

On your slight shins.

And your lack of stature in your own estimation

Has put you on higher heels
Than the dance requires.

And you trip early
Before the music plays.

And the terror of things falling
Reminds you
There is so much to clear away
To do away with
To run away from
Before the night falls.

Push aside the terror of things to be done
For the blind beggar is calling
He is calling out to the Son of David
Whom he cannot see
But whom he knows, he hears
Is passing by.

And the wild clamour of his ardent anguish
Cannot be smothered
By the hostile crowd.

He is losing hope at the terror of people crushing him

But the Master stops

For him alone

And tells him to

Draw near.


And the crowd turns to the seated man

'Courage, Bartimeus,

He is calling you!'

And the cloak that protects him

He flings aside

And he runs

In his personal darkness

To the Lord who waits.


Push aside the terror of things to be done

There is nothing to be done

But to hear Him

Asking

'What do you want of me?'

The One by whom all things can be done.


And the beggar,

Wise, in his reckless trust

Begs now for the gift of sight.

And Jesus, son of David

Has pity on him
And says 'Go' for the Light has come.
'Your faith has healed you'.
The dark has gone
And his eyes receive the sun.

And Bartimeus accompanies Him
Along the road
At once.
The terror at last is pushed aside.
The winter is over
And gone.


Sarah de Nordwall    October 24th and 25th 2009
*Inspired by the title of a poem (of the same title) by Pope
John Paul II and by Fr Antonio Ritaccio sermon on
Bartimeus

**34.**

I love the idea of inner journeys – of voyages and returns that take one beyond oneself and into the heart of things. This is why we are nearly all of us entranced by wardrobes into Narnia, journeys to visit sea princesses that last one hundred earth years, and a simple stepping through the looking glass into Wonderland. But more is meant by this than mere escapism. A myth is hereby summoned that feeds a longing that seems utterly native to our heart. And why would we have so deep a longing if it had no use or origin, no possibility of fulfilment? It is important to notice the doorways. Poets are there for that very purpose.

**This is my Gift**

This is my gift
It's a honeysuckle blossom
If you breathe her in
All your sadness disappears instantly
For ever
Till the next time you need her.

She has an infinite horizon inside her
But she lives in time

And all her shores extend to emerald seas
And you can stand upon her shores
And dive into her oceans when you please.

You'll find there almost everything you've longed for
But you know you must return

But how you are when you return
Is wholly up to you.

This is my gift
To you.


December 2014

**35.**

Now, speaking of gifts, how can I have forgotten an old boss I had who was so transparently eloquent when it came to talking about women, or should I say, lamenting? Because he was always wondering why he could so easily find a girlfriend but not a wife. Eager to be of assistance, I asked him to explain. And this is pretty much word for word, what he said.

### I need a More Old Fashioned Girl

I need a more old-fashioned girl
But she'd better not be thick
Cos she needs to read my every mood
And know what makes me tick.

I want her quite dependent
So I'll know I'm truly needed
But if she takes up too much time
Her pleas might go unheeded

Cos I need some space
I need her near
I need her to be home

But now, she's always in the house
I need some time alone.

But she mustn't get too independent
Though she has to be happy when left
Cos there's nothing more draining than women who say
That without you they're simply bereft

But the women you meet these days
Seem to traipse about in a herd
Now, I grew out of that in my 20s
And at 30 it just looks absurd.

And she's got to be a match for me
But she'd better not try to compete
And she'd better be clever
But not more than me
Or that might make me feel incomplete.

Most of all, she must not be aggressive.
That's just so unattractive to see.
Oh there must be a woman who's docile and bright
And yet wholly attracted to me.

And I'll let her be somewhat successful.

Well, she's got to have something to say
But if she is over dynamic
Then she'll probably get in the way.

So, maybe I'll go to the library
I'll just wander down for a look
For a nice quiet woman who's eager to learn
If there's none I'll just get out a book.

So at least I can daydream
Until the great day
When the perfect, compliant one
Sidles my way
With a singular mission and just this to say
That she's here, but to worship, to love and obey.

Yes, she'll truly admire and adore me
And yet know who exactly I am
For illusions are dangerous.

Facts are much worse.
It is truly so hard,
Being a man.

**36.**

Of course it's so much easier being a woman! And we are so much more easy to please;

**The Freedom Safety Fantasy**

Keep me safe
But leave me free
Stay close by
But let me be.

Do what I want but don't be docile
I'm not attracted to a victim profile.
Make me feel I'm strong and sorted.
Isn't it nice to be escorted?

Read my silence
Speak your mind
Get me excited
Let me unwind

Give me the thrill
Of a passion that's implied.
Show me that you care for me
With love you cannot hide.


Give me a sense of mystery:
The poetics of the seer.
Make it plain you need me
Just to take away my fear

And then I'll give you all my love
But guard my heart with care.
How freeing to be trusting,
How prudent to beware!


1997

**37.**

In my quest for the solution to these easy-to-recognise paradoxes, I have discovered a particular doorway that also shares a narrative with the Bridegroom and the Bride. This poem came one morning after a memorable trip to Jerusalem, where I uncovered and experienced a renewed sense of the meaning of rest on Sunday, or as it was in the Jewish world, the Sabbath, from Friday night to Saturday at sunset. It became a doorway to the most beautiful enchantment of all.

**Show me the Door!**

If you knew
There was a temple made of time
Which held a mystery

A day made of eternity

Wouldn't you be racing
Aching for more
Asking every passer-by
"Show me the door!"

If you knew

That a land where life was new

Flowed with delight


And crowned at its height

With a wedding banquet


Was waiting for you

And that you had a passport

But needed no transport

Wouldn't you cry out all the more

"Show me the door!"


If you knew

That the One who made all

Opened a skylight


Let in the moonlight

When the bell tolled


And all was transformed there

Rooted and grew there

Into its true self

Learnt to be free

Wouldn't you beg to be offered the key?

You know the alleyway
You know the wall

You know the songs to sing
You know the call

You know the dances
Come take the floor!

Angels of Sabbath
Stand

Here at the door.


March 27th 2013

## 38.

And once inside, there is an end to striving, if such a discipline can be embraced, in which joy is commanded and one must feast three times! I witnessed it in Jerusalem, at the Friday night meal of a Rabbi, (who opened his house each week, to whoever wished to enter) and I also experienced it at the house of the Hirsch family in Mea Sherim. They greeted each other with the gentle greeting of the Yiddish word 'Shabbos', pronounced 'Shabbis'. And the delight was utterly palpable. I returned home after the feast and wrote the following two poems.

**I have waited**

I have waited till beauty
Was restored to me
Before I built my house.

I intuited her presence
Through her absence
The texture and flow
Of her possibilities.

Without her

No construction would be meaningful

No field fertile

And no orchard blossoming.


I waited until beauty

Was restored to me

Before I built my house.


What leads the heart to know homecoming?

Only the one who calls.


What leads the heart

To seek till she find Him?

Surely the One who builds.


I waited till beauty

Was restored to me

For without her

No life could be


And He who builds

Restored my soul

And the Palace of Time He gave me.

No things were changed

Yet all was transformed

I entered the
Temple of Rest

And joy resided
Where He had decided
We lived in a time
That was blessed.

No land was required
To structure this home
The hours were the fabric
Of bliss.

I waited till beauty
Had spoken her name

That mine might be new
Ah Shabbos!

June 2010

**39.**

**Be my Guest**

Fortitude, Prudence, Temperance, Justice
My four strong sisters
Thank you for your aid
But now, I ask you with a simple grace
To stop and sit down at the Sabbath Gate.

Put down your tools
And breathe before you enter
For something greater than yourselves is here.

And it is He who will refresh you
He who will provide
He who will require no payment
He who will preside.

Fortitude, courageous heart
Your rest is here prepared
And Prudence, all your careful plans
So wise, let them be aired.

Temperance, here is your command;

Three feasts you must enjoy - desire!
Then taste my gift for Justice
Which will draw us near the fire;

Mercy, vintage from the vine of grace.
Within this ecstasy find your place.

Let me be the fresh creation
Let me now create in you
Let me be the Lord Sabaoth
Joy is all there is to do!

In this time, you feast in Holiness.
Work, production, let them be!
Here we are now at the Centre
I in you and you in Me.

Rest, Spontaneity, Festival, Mercy,
Kiss your sisters, lest they pine!
Fortitude, Prudence, Temperance, Justice
We've revived you, just in Time.

June 2010

**40.**

I was in a café in London not long ago and I was musing on the blissful experience of homecoming that cafés can bring and I wondered about this lovely phrase 'a spirit of Sabbath'. I'd asked someone how the rabbi could afford to give about fifty people such a wonderful meal every single week. 'Ah' they said, as if it required no further explanation, 'He does it in a Spirit of Sabbath'. 'Ah' I said. What an abundant attitude! Indeed. It flows from beyond, from the One who gives all.

**Café Come Home**

In a café
You can be light-hearted
About the tragedies of the world.

Cos you've come home

And in the soul place
Everyone's done OK
Enough

And the struggle, for now

Is over

You're in the boat

You smile at a fellow conspirator
At a nearby table

But not for long
Because you mustn't let on:
We're all happy here!
No one must know!

*Look, stop right there, you tell me*
*Enough of this*
*Preposterous self-satisfaction*
*Don't you know there's a war on?*

Where?

*Everywhere, never stops, never will.*

Then have pause, I say
For some soul satisfaction.
You might return a glimmer
Wiser

To the great debacle

The sliding into the abyss

Tobogganing into the yawning chaos

*There you go again, you say*

*All this reckless disregard for demise*

*And universal urgency*

I yawn in anticipation of the next onslaught.

Then feel ashamed and cough

I blame it on my Jewish ancestry I explain

By way of sociological excuse

All those commands to rest and feast, you know

Refusals to mourn in the face of death

To sing of the Sabbath of Contentment

Within earshot of the battle cry.

I order a chocolate cornflake crispy thing for your coffee

So we can sing our own Kiddush

But you aren't convinced

*'I could make one of those at home*

*For two and a half p!' you cry*

Indignant

'But you haven't'
I reply
And you relent.

I smile.
We smile.

No one can convince me
And I never can convince myself,
That I don't have any money
In a café

Cos in a soul space
Abundance reigns.


31st July 2012

**41.**

Yes indeed. Some things in life are simply sacred and need to be preserved, as such. This is why I feel passionately about the taking of laptops into this graced arena.

**On why one feels reluctant to take a laptop into a café**

Maybe it wasn't accidentally
That I left my laptop at the counter
Before entering the café.

Like taking ones shoes off before entering the mosque
And hanging your coat at the door,

A café requires divestment.
Here, only soul tools should be utilised –

Papyrus may be allowed.

Those roughly woven pieces of Nile-soaked *Cyperus*, that we
learnt about at school

By dint of which vegetable matter,
And diligent, sideways-sitting scribes

We heard the ancient stories from deep time.

You may bring vellum

Or that Chinese innovation,
Grasped at eagerly by Renaissance artists;
Paper, which they made from ropes and sails.

How glorious that on the detritus of seafaring vessels,
Bound with trading plans across the burgeoning world

They sketched with silver the incarnate God
And His mummy holding him this and that way;
Fra Lippo Lippi and da Vinci, with a thousand repetitions
and re-visitings
Hoping to penetrate the mystery.

So paper is allowed.

But pixelled plastic and her alien lights
Are not as elemental as we need.

Perhaps an iPhone made of bronze
A laptop set with lapis lazuli, inlaid in rosewood
And with marble keys

We might consider these
If the marquetry is fine;
The inlaid pearl exquisite
And the on-light green with emerald or citrine.

Essentially, you're best to bring
A simple slate with chalk.

A cuniform stylus and a soft clay block
Are also known to talk.

We find the energy we need
Is not the electric kind

In every café
Where the soul sings free
The laptop
Is left behind.

**42.**

So cafés are a natural vehicle for the numinous - conveyances for the bounty of the world - and so are trains. Nothing yet surpasses the romance of train travel down a British coastline. Along one of my favourite routes to beautiful Edinburgh up the East Coast, I looked out of the window and suddenly saw the sea.

**The Coastal Robot**

Incredible how the sea dispels alarm

And breaks through city anguish
Arouses joy without a cause
Immediate.

A sight of bliss so inarticulate
And yet replete with messages and thrones.

Then suddenly a monstrous thing
A squat and hideous robot, square and brute
Sits on the coast line like an ugly toy left out by troll children
Blind to the ravishing waves.

A factory made of concrete blocks.

A nuclear power station?

What exactly is it?

Could one possibly say

Without initiation into madness of the bluntest kind?


And there and here beside the railway tracks

Vast cylinders and wagons,

Making grey a frightful thing


Whilst the veiling mist attempts a kind reminder of the

Truthful nature of this

Heavenly shade, so close to silver and to dawn.


But peace,

The breath returns and someone with a gentle eye has now

Laid out the land


A green field

Of a generous startling hue


Gives us a barn

With a long bright roof of red.


A white house by a fallow field

And a crimson post van in a country lane.

Its speed commensurate with human dignity
And a sense of pace of life.

Oh Lord protect us from the pace-less things
That sit enthroned in deathless tedium.

Rip out the horrors that can never breathe
And fill again our earth with life that dies
And naturally expires in rapturous gratitude.

How wonderful that things ephemeral
Lift up our fragile hopes into eternity.

Whilst stolid robots stiff with glass-eyed potency
Will changeless, fall entire into the night.


April 2012

**43.**

## The Angel Coast or Unexpected gold

Bright heaven has let down her guard
And falls bedazzled on the winter sea.

The torrent breakers grey and wild
Erupt in scintillating cries of light

Bright platinum flashing white and
Flecked with unexpected gold.

How came this glorious gift
To such a cold stone shore?

The whitening chalk cliffs, tender
Honoured yet, breathe phantom like and mute

Beside excoriating power volcanic
Bursting from the home of light
In unrelenting bliss.

Kiss now our homely earth
And fling your star falls in the lucid air

As throngs of birds in undulating joy

Pitch up
And fall
And rise again
Against the anguish of the blistering gales

Leaving with the myriad plays of light.
Lightless birds, heightening the air with cries

Fine soundings of an infinite wealth
Of time
And turning space

Frothed and breakered
In the drenching roar of sound.

Out far beyond the realm of all our pinpoint
Shore-bound possibility
This too much turmoil of unmeasurable beauty
Pierces forth in
Unreciprocal power.

Unending and unbearable glory

Tears and sweeps away

The last of all my heart's defences

Till all this so

Unmeasured glory

Enters in.


2002

**44.**

**Holy Saturday Streets**

Inside me

Are the streets of Jerusalem.

Sun on the old stone stairways

And the baking air.


Inside me

Are the high walls and the tumbling flowers,

Vivid as a clarion call in a net of leaves,

Red and pink in the thorns and prickles.


Even the plants must arm themselves

Against the night and the harsh demands of day

And yet it is always the sunshine that persists,

Delights my inner eye.

I feel the peace of Sabbath streets

Within me.

The Jewish Quarter vertical with praise.

The men are hurrying to meet the Bride.

They circle with a dance of joy by the Temple wall

As the night falls

*It is already night when joy begins*

*The Sabbath is at hand and a beautifying surplus of soul*

*Visits our mortal bones and lingers on.*

A Light of Resurrection

A climate of unchangeable joy

And I rejoice in the springing up

Of the eternal tale.

He walked and spoke and lived

He died and rose again.

These streets bear testament to His being here.

The bells of the Triduum ring.

We hurry to the Russian church.

The tapering candles held

To the glimmering faces of the radiant saints.

The choir from Moscow sings

Deep-throated harmonies at the very gates of hell.

These Christ has touched by His all Perfect Presence

His all-emptying Praise.

Obedience calls him to so great, so vast, to such abysmal fall

Descent

And yet a royal progress through the chaos of the soul

Man's soul and deeds since sin first entered in,

Commenced its tearing and dismembering work,

Enacted by the hands of men.

He walks there now

A world more vast than all the earth's globe utterly destroyed

And still He has no power to ascend.

He walks and powerless he waits

Till there alone the Easter dawn appears.


A flake of light

As gentle as a solitary leaf

Falls like a kiss upon the metal hell of death


A forest full of leaves of light blow in like a rivening flame

The second chaos soars with hope

Breaks forth with a roar of joy


Who is this King of Glory?

O, lift Higher Ancient Doors!

And let Him enter, Who has come

To claim and take us home!


21st February 2013

**45.**

## I Don't have Time to Think about the Resurrection

*Prologue*

I don't have time to think about the Resurrection.

Having successfully spent a significant proportion of my time
Constructing essential boundaries,
I don't need someone suddenly walking through the wall.

Is it polite?
What's a door for?

Honestly some people have no manners
No sense of appropriate behaviour

I don't want people
Breathing on me.

It's simply rude.

I don't need someone else's air
I just want my own space in which to breathe.

I need my individuality kept intact

And the walls keep the roof on, thankyou

And the sky

Is for outside

Not inside my house.

I like the heating turned up

And the door closed.

*Part Two*

One day I was walking

Not far from the house

And a man approached silently.

I hardly noticed him there

But he spoke quietly

And asked a simple question

'Where are you going?'

I wasn't sure, but he came along anyway.

'Haven't you heard the news?' I asked.

He seemed interested in my take on it.

I explained to him how everything was a complete disaster.

We came to a friend's house and I made a suggestion.

Mother would have been scandalised, but not my Gran;

I invited him in for supper - a stranger

And it was then I noticed something:

I can't exactly tell you what.

He seemed different somehow

As we said the blessing

No, not exactly different

In fact quite the reverse

It was as though I'd known Him all my life.

He was the most familiar person in the world.

I was taken aback.

He smiled.

Here was the person I had so very long been looking for

And here he was

Impossible

Incredible

A breaking in of light.

I promise you

I stood there marvelling

My heart for a moment full of sunshine

And suddenly

He was gone

Like the sun disappearing behind a cloud

The shock of the chill

But you now don't doubt

The existence of the sun.


I ran out of the house

And back the way we'd come

At triple speed

Was he somewhere waiting?

No, I knew it was greater than this.


I ran and ran under an open sky

Back to the City

Back to the place of alleyways and winding streets

And when I found my door

I flung it open


And they were there inside

They'd seen him too

We knew


What did we know?

Our joy exploded
Suddenly all of us only
And everywhere
Only had time
To think about the Resurrection.

And the walls were laughing
And the roof was off
People who passed by
Asked us to close the door
To keep the noise of the singing in.
They didn't have time for a party

And how we laughed and hoped they would
And some of them came in
To hear the news.

The roof
The roof was off.

26<sup>th</sup> April 2015

**46.**

I discovered that the Greek word from which therapy is derived, has three related meanings – to honour the gods, to cultivate a garden, and healing. The idea of this inspired this poem after a wonderful creative weekend in the ancient town of Rye and after a Prayer and Art day with Sr. Sheila Gosney on the subject of gardens.

**Tending Paradise**

**Part One – God Speaks**

You are too frightened to enter my garden.
I think you fight the tangles in your own.

I cannot rush the thorn trees in a frenzy
You'd only find your own heart
Bruised and torn.

And so I wait alone and think of a garden
The garden that I tended long ago
Before we met.

## Part Two – Confession

I saw an old man
Or so I thought

Thin and tall
Enter the wooden door.

I only saw his back
And the long brown robe.

I entered through another door and knelt
At the lattice gate.

He was waiting
Silent
His eyes turned from me
Closed
His ear attentive

He was very young
He looked like a King.

The finest features
The most poised of profiles.

What African country
He had come from
I could not identify.

I told Him all that
Was on my heart.

Through all
My tangles
He waited
Deeply.

I had the full attention of the King.

'My sister', he said

(Such unexpected words,
So natural to Him,
An accent I had never heard)

'These are very complex issues.
Who can tell where one life ends
And another person's life
Begins?

We live so often in the
Face of near
Impossibility

But we can persevere'.


He took them one by one,
The stones from the dry path.

'Think of the great Teresa,
Even she, who felt she knew
What she was called by God to do
Was often faced with
Insurmountable difficulties.

But we can know, my sister,
When we pray, that God can
Open a window
and we see things suddenly
in a wholly new
and unexpected way'.

## Part three – To Cultivate a Garden

When we were little
We would make Japanese Gardens
Out of a tea tray and a jam jar lid.

The tray we'd fill with soil,
Moss from the trees would be grass
And gravely stones, the garden path.

Twigs would be trees
And the bright round jam lid filled with water
Was a shining pond.

How proud we were of our minute creations!
What delight they gave us

As imaginary birds
Drank from the water source.

We were queens of a greening realm
That smelt of earth.

And all the blossoms we would fling in showers
Would fill our gardens with a feast of flowers.

## Part four – A Process of Healing

The town of Rye is crowned by a tower,
A stronghold from the eleven hundreds.
Fortress-strong for a thousand years,
It stood against the French and other brash invasions,
from rough raiders to wild pirates
And the odd rum-smuggling poor.


Within its walls they built a woman's prison
Where, on bread and water and a Bible diet
They would do penance for their crime of being poor and
Having stepped outside the rules designed by men,
And men with money too, let's note.


But just outside the prison door
Another than a jailor's hand
had planted a herb garden
In the ancient style.

And from the look-out in the
Unforgiving tower
I looked down on the garden and the jail

And wondered at the strange arrangement.

There, in early spring
In winds awash with storms
No fragrance rose from the green plants
Vying with the over-riding dearth.

The brown and tangles
Far surpassed the green
But round the plants a trellis framework stood
And made a shelter
That lent hope a shape.

Did they in Victorian years
In summer days, peer out
From the dour jail
And breathe in air.. the marjoram and rue
The rosemary and lavender.

Remorse and wild impossibility,
Stone impasse and the scent of flowers.

Vulgar laughter in the cell and tower
As those despairing of a life of justice

Jibe at fate and make

A joke of dreams.


And yet I wonder

If the garden grew

In such proximity

That their gaze could fall

On something loved and tended

Though so small


And if they knew

a rustling or a savour


Of the One who tends the medicine

For the Fall.


April 2014

**47.**

Poems often come in pairs, like a diptych, to help one understand. These were written in Lent, the day after my father's interment of ashes, just after breakfast, when my friend Tom noticed that the leaves on the cherry boughs had at last appeared.

**This is my Easter**

This is my Easter
It came early this year,
Earlier than everyone else's,
Like a private Spring.

And there were young leaves
On the cherry-tree bough
Miraculously green in the light
In the sitting room
And the house was a place
Of transfiguration.

And it was you who saw it first,
Like a Herald of the New Evangelisation
In between breakfast and washing up;
Afternoon duties broken open into a flowering horizon.

And I will go out now
After so much death
Has blossomed like the spring brightness,

cold and clear,
Into a surrounding presence

And whichever way I walk now
It will be
Towards you
In eternity

And this is freedom.


## When we forgive

When we forgive,
We build a garden
For other people to live in.

They may be far away
But as they are walking
Alone in a distant wood
They will look up
And see a bird,
Which suddenly they hear
As though a new sense had been given to them

And there, inside their heart
A new dimension of their inner landscape
Will appear
Like the birth of a new world
Instantly

And like water flowing from the rock
And waterfalls from high and verdant cliffs
The sound of a rising torrent now will not alarm them,
For a world of danger is a world of life
And all we ask for is a high adventure.

When we forgive
We give birth to worlds.

Had we imagined that we had such power within
To bring delight
And all of it so new, we stand amazed?

For we, the lesser gods
Are not the origin
But through us pours
The gift 'originality',

Which, to behold, we wonder and give praise
To Him, whose mercy made so wide a freedom.
And I who am forgiven
Wear my crown.

1st March 2015

**48.**

## Part of me is Not Tormented

Part of me is not tormented.
It's the part where you live
The neighbourhood you moved into
And pulled the blinds up

And put boxes of geraniums in the windows.
Then everyone did the same
And some put a jasmine tree on the front lawn
And others put a bay tree on the front porch.

I remember, I opened the window
And the air was full of promise.

Part of me is not tormented.
It's the part that woke up when you came round
Knocked on the door
In the middle of a difficult moment
And you led away the perpetrator.
'I'll take care of this' you said
And I trusted you
And both of us were relieved.

I sat down in a quiet chair and breathed.

Part of me is not tormented.
It's the part that has a sign over the door saying
Welcome!
Where you persuaded me
To open a theatre
Not for surgery exactly
But for plays called
Transformation is an operation
You can perform!
We don't call it that.

You play the main role
And we just celebrate.

I love everything about it
Even putting the dishes away
After the ice cream and the gingerbread is all gone
And the guests are all asleep at home.

Part of me is not tormented
And the last rites
When the final shadow
Exited stage left with a dramatic cry

Were merely a prelude
To a great night of poetry and stars.

How terrible that so many have dared to pin
The torments of life on You.

When all You do is step with Light and newness
Into the neighbourhood
Till all the torments are no longer to be found
But on the road out of town
Hunting for a place to dwell
Where you do not.

None of me is now tormented
Because
You
Rule.

3rd June 2015

**49.**

For all this beautiful healing work to fully take root in the garden of our souls and the architecture of our neighbourhood, I still find that the Sabbath that is 'fenced in as if with roses' is key. Now, for Christians, it has blossomed into the resurrected glory of the $8^{th}$ day. It has become the Day of the Lord, when the 'evolutionary leap', as Pope Benedict calls it, of the Resurrection, has taken place and we have been given a glimpse of who we shall be, when all time ceases and we come to the great crossroads of eternity.

Here then is the fresh reason to stop and receive, to put our faith in the pure delight of the dance to come and achieve the quiet revolution.

**The Quiet Revolution**

Again the Sabbath comes to mind
Why?
Because it's quiet while God works
It's an act of faith
The stillness
The not going anywhere

Not doing anything to make a visible change

You're just existing

But existing's good

And that's the point.


The Quiet Revolution

Is a discipline of mind

An opening of the heart

Because the peace is all around.


It's an act of hope

The listening

Not saying too much

Not expecting thoughts to change essence of the world.


It's a time of praise

For all that was before you came

And all that will be when you're gone.


It's an act of love

Of the world around you

In which the present troubles disappear

And all that matters is the great Shalom

Which now you enter in

Because you've chosen

To choose this pearl
Above all other things.
And there you feel the Quiet Revolution,
The silken pearl within your upturned palm.
Such beauty will not know a diminution
But change from glory unto glorious psalm.


2013

**50.**

And so we come to the end of the '50 poems for my 50$^{th}$' Birthday Party collection, and in the tradition of all good comedies, we should end, as we shall hope to do at the end of all things, with a dance. For as Tom Kingsley Jones once said in the Bard Library in Bayswater, 'I imagine that we dance into heaven.' And suddenly it seemed perfectly possible, that one day we should all be together and all things should be well; dancing into heaven.


**Dancing into Heaven**

Like the arrival
Of Cosmic Harmony
At the end of the comedy,
There must be dancing into heaven.

The point of the story,
Where all roads open
Into infinite possibility
Is where we begin

Via the backward steps

Into a glorious twist

Turns and spins
And beats just missed
Yet all can be recovered in the final mix.

So there must be dancing in a celebration
To catch the rhythm of the innovation
That brings us together for the final embarkation.

And even in the deepest silence
We'll find there was music all the way

Accompanying us by night and day
As we danced alone and in every weather
Dancing together
Into heaven.

8th June 2015
The Bard Library, St Mary of the Angels, Bayswater, London.